JESUS CALLING BIBLE STUDY SERIES

RECEIVING CHRIST'S HOPE

8 SESSIONS

Sarah Young

with Karen Lee-Thorp

THOMAS NELSON
Since 1798

NASHVILLE   MEXICO CITY   RIO DE JANEIRO

Published in Nashville, Tennessee, by Nelson Books, an imprint of Thomas Nelson. Nelson Books and Thomas Nelson are registered trademarks of HarperCollins Christian Publishing, Inc.

All Scripture quotations, unless otherwise indicated, are taken from The Holy Bible, *New International Version*®, NIV®. Copyright © 1973, 1978, 1984, 2011 by Biblica, Inc.® Used by permission. All rights reserved worldwide.

Scripture quotations marked NKJV are taken from the New King James Version. Copyright © 1982 by Thomas Nelson, Inc. Used by permission. All rights reserved.

Scripture quotations marked ESV are taken from *The Holy Bible, English Standard Version,* copyright © 2001 by Crossway Bibles, a division of Good News Publishers. Used by permission. All rights reserved.

ISBN 978-0-7180-3589-1

First Printing May 2015 / Printed in the United States of America

CONTENTS

INTRODUCTION

Sometimes our busy and difficult lives give us the impression that God is silent. We cry out to Him, but our feelings tell us that He isn't answering our prayers. In this, our feelings are incorrect. God hears our prayers and speaks right into the situations in which we find ourselves. The trouble is that our lives are often too hectic, our minds too distracted, for us to take in what God offers.

This *Jesus Calling* Bible study is designed to help individuals and groups meditate on the words of Scripture and hear them not just as words said to people long ago but as words said to us today in the here and now. The goal is to help the heart hear and respond to what the mind reads. We want to encounter the living God as He speaks through the Scriptures. The writer to the Hebrews tells us:

In the past God spoke to our ancestors through the prophets at many times and in various ways, but in these last days he has spoken to us by his Son, whom he appointed heir of all things, and through whom also he made the universe. The Son is the radiance of God's glory and the exact representation of his being, sustaining all things by his powerful word.

—HEBREWS 1:1–3

God has spoken to us through His Son, Jesus Christ. The New Testament gives us the chance to walk with Jesus, see what He does, and hear Him speak into the sometimes confusing situations in which we find ourselves. The Old Testament tells us the story of how God prepared a people to be the family of Jesus, and in the experiences of those men and women we find our own lives mirrored.

THE GOAL OF THIS SERIES

The *Jesus Calling Bible Study Series* offers you a chance to lay down your cares, enter God's Presence, and hear Him speak through His Word. You will get to spend some time in silence studying a passage of Scripture, and if you're meeting with a group, you'll get to share your insights and hear what others discovered. You'll also get to discuss excerpts from the *Jesus Calling* devotional that relate to the themes of the Bible passages. In this way, you will learn how to better make space in your life for the Spirit of God to speak to you through the Word of God and the people of God.

THE FLOW OF EACH SESSION

Each session of this study guide contains the following elements:

- CONSIDER IT. The one or two questions in this opening section serve as an icebreaker to help you start to think about the theme of the session. These questions will help you connect the theme to your own past or present experience and will help you get to know the others in your group more deeply. If you've had a busy day and your mind is full of distractions, this section will help you better focus.

- EXPERIENCE IT. Here you will find two readings from *Jesus Calling* along with some questions for reflection. This is your chance to talk with others about the biblical principles found within the *Jesus Calling* devotions. Can you relate to what each reading describes? What insights from God's Word does it illuminate? What does it motivate you to do? This section will help you apply these biblical principles to your everyday habits.

- STUDY IT. Next you'll explore one or two Scripture passages connected to the session topic and the readings from *Jesus Calling*. You will not only analyze these passages but also pray through them in ways designed to engage your heart as well as your head. You'll first talk with your group about what the passage means and then spend several minutes in silence, letting God speak into your own life through His Word.

- LIVE IT. Finally, you will find five days' worth of suggested Scripture passages that you can pray through on your own during the week. Suggested questions for additional study and reflection are provided.

FOR LEADERS

If you are leading a group through this study guide, please see the Leader's Notes at the end of the guide. You'll find background on the design of the study as well as suggested answers for some of the study questions.

OUR HOPE IS
FUTURE-DIRECTED

CONSIDER IT

Have you heard of the Slow Food movement? Slow Fooders believe good food is worth waiting for. Founded in 1986 as an alternative to fast food, the movement encourages people to cook more traditional fare that takes time and isn't made in a factory.

Slow Food goes against the grain of our microwave culture. We like instant food and instant messages. We hate to wait. This is what often makes hope hard for us, because hope is about waiting. If we hope for something, we are longing for what we don't yet have. Nobody hopes for what they already have.

Biblical hope is a bit different from the way we use *hope* in everyday conversation. In ordinary talk you might say, "I hope you feel better," or, "I hope I'll have a better job someday," or, "I haven't given up hope for my football team, even though they've lost three games." In these instances hope means a wish; something we want to happen but don't necessarily have confidence about. Or it means positive thinking, with the idea that thinking alone can make something happen.

When the biblical writers use the word, however, they mean something different. They're talking about something they long for and are solidly confident of getting. It's not just positive thinking. It's confidence. Yet even though biblical hope is confident waiting, it's *still* waiting. And we don't like that.

In this first session, we'll dive into biblical hope and consider whether the hope offered in the Bible is genuinely worth waiting for.

1. *Name three things you long for but don't yet have. How confident are you of getting those things? Why?*

_____

_____

_____

_____

EXPERIENCE IT

"Softly I announce My Presence. Shimmering hues of radiance tap gently at your consciousness, seeking entrance. Though I have all Power in heaven and on earth, I am infinitely tender with you. The weaker you are, the more gently I approach you. Let your weakness be a door to My Presence. Whenever you feel inadequate, remember that I am your *ever-present Help*. Hope in Me, and you will be protected from depression and self-pity. Hope is like a golden cord connecting you to heaven. The more you cling to this cord, the more I bear the weight of your burdens; thus, you are lightened. Heaviness is not of My kingdom. Cling to hope, and My rays of Light will reach you through the darkness."

—FROM *JESUS CALLING*, JANUARY 8

2. *What do you think it means to say that hope is "like a golden cord connecting you to heaven"?*

3. *What are the benefits of placing your hope in God? What has been your experience of these benefits, or how would you like to experience them?*

"Waiting, trusting, and hoping are intricately connected, like golden strands interwoven to form a strong chain. Trusting is the central strand, because it is the response from My children that I desire the most. Waiting and hoping embellish the central strand and strengthen the chain that connects you to Me. Waiting for Me to work, with your eyes on Me, is evidence that you really do trust Me. If you mouth the words 'I trust You' while anxiously trying to make things go your way, your words ring hollow. Hoping is future-directed, connecting you to your inheritance in heaven. However, the benefits of hope fall fully on you in the present. Because you are Mine, you don't just pass time in your waiting. You can wait expectantly, in hopeful trust. Keep your 'antennae' out to pick up even the faintest glimmer of My Presence."

—FROM *JESUS CALLING*, MARCH 12

4. *How does hope connect you to your inheritance in heaven? Why is it important to attach your hopes to that inheritance rather than to things on earth?*

5. *What are the present benefits of future-directed hope? How would you like to experience those benefits more fully?*

STUDY IT

Read aloud the following passage from Romans 8:18–25. In these verses, the apostle Paul encourages his readers to persevere in living their faith in spite of the sufferings of this life.

I consider that our present sufferings are not worth comparing with the glory that will be revealed in us. For the creation waits in eager expectation for the children of God to be revealed. For the creation was subjected to frustration, not by its own choice, but by the will of the one who subjected it, in hope that the creation itself will be liberated from its bondage to decay and brought into the freedom and glory of the children of God.

We know that the whole creation has been groaning as in the pains of childbirth right up to the present time. Not only so, but we ourselves, who have the firstfruits of the Spirit, groan inwardly as we wait eagerly for our adoption to sonship, the redemption of our bodies. For in this hope we were saved. But hope that is seen is no hope at all. Who hopes for what they already have? But if we hope for what we do not yet have, we wait for it patiently.

6. *The apostle Paul says the creation itself "waits in eager expectation" for something. What is the creation waiting for? In what sense have the children of God not yet been "revealed"?*

7. *What are some ways in which the creation is currently in "bondage to decay"?*

8. *Paul says we "groan inwardly" as we wait eagerly for "the redemption of our bodies." What will the redemption of our bodies be? What will it be like to have a redeemed body?*

9. *Paul says "hope that is seen is no hope at all." What does that mean to you? How does it help you understand what hope is?*

10. *Read the passage aloud again. Take two minutes of silence to reread the passage, looking for a sentence, phrase, or even one word that stands out as something Jesus wants you to hear. Ask Him to help you hear Him. If you're meeting with a group, the leader will keep track of time. At the end of two minutes, you may share with the group the word or phrase that came to you in the silence.*

11. *Read the passage aloud again. Take two minutes of silence, asking Jesus what He is saying to you through the word or phrase you selected and whether He would like you to do anything in response. If you're meeting with a group, the leader will again keep track of time. At the end of two minutes, you may share with the group what came to you in the silence if you wish.*

12. *What was it like for you to sit in silence with the passage? Did soaking in the passage like this help you take it in better than before?*

13. *If you're meeting with a group, how can the members pray for you? If you're using this study on your own, what would you like to say to God right now?*

LIVE IT

At the end of each session you'll find suggested Scripture readings for spending time alone with God during five days of the coming week. Each day of this week's readings will deal with the theme of waiting in hope. Read each passage slowly, pausing to think about what is being said. Rather than approaching this as an assignment to complete, think of it as an opportunity to meet with a Person. Use any of the questions that are helpful.

Day 1

Read Romans 8:26–27. What help do we get from the Holy Spirit during this time of hopeful waiting? Why is this helpful?

Do you ever have "wordless groans" when you pray? Explain.

How does the Holy Spirit's activity help you wait with patience? How hard is it for you currently to wait with patience?

Express your hope and your need to the Holy Spirit in a prayer.

Day 2

Read Romans 8:28–30. What do Paul's words in this passage add to your understanding of what you are waiting for?

What does it mean to be "conformed to the image of his [God's] Son"?

How does being conformed to the image of Christ help you wait with patience and hope?

Are there any things in your life that cause you to question whether God is working in them for your good? If so, talk with Him about those things. Ask Him to confidently and patiently strengthen your hope as He conforms you to the image of His Son.

Day 3

Read Lamentations 3:19–23. What affliction do you remember? Is your soul ever downcast because of it?

Why does the author of this passage say he has hope despite his bitter memories?

Do his words give you hope? Why or why not?

_____

_____

_____

Think of some examples of how the Lord's compassions are new every morning. Take some time to be honest with Him about your memories and to thank Him for today's compassions.

Day 4

Read Lamentations 3:24–29. What does it mean to say the Lord is your portion?

_____

_____

_____

Is that an abundant portion or a meager portion? Why?

_____

_____

_____

_____

Do you believe the Lord is good to those whose hope is in Him? What evidence do you have?

What does it mean to "bear the yoke" (verse 27)? How can the author say that is a good thing when it's so difficult?

Do you trust the Lord enough to sit in silence with a heavy weight on your shoulders if He has put it there? Talk with Him about this.

Day 5

Read Lamentations 3:30–33. What reasons for hope does the author offer?

What does "unfailing love" mean?

_____

_____

_____

_____

How has the Lord treated you with unfailing love?

_____

_____

_____

_____

*Does it help you to know the Lord doesn't willingly (with pleasure) bring
affliction on anyone? If He doesn't enjoy it and has the power to prevent it, why
does He bring it?*

_____

_____

_____

_____

Ask God to strengthen you to endure with patience whatever affliction
you have. Also ask Him to help you have hope in His unfailing love.

OUR HOPE IS IN GOD'S PRESENCE

CONSIDER IT

All too often our hopes are attached to things that are good but not *ultimately* good. We hope for good health, or for successful and obedient children, or for a happy marriage, or for an interesting job, or for enough money to retire. While God may grant these things, none of them are guaranteed. Rather, God invites us to hope for what is ultimately good: Himself. He invites us to know Him intimately and become like Him. If we attach our hopes to God, we will never be disappointed.

We get a taste of God's Presence in this life as we spend more and more time with Him, knowing the ultimate fulfillment of our hope will come in heaven. While this hope of heaven can feel far away and vague, we can be gripped by it here and now through the glimpses of it we find in God's Word. We are meant to start entering into the ways of heaven now, and when our heavenly hope becomes substantive and real to us, it is easier to hold our earthly hopes with a more relaxed hand.

In this session we'll take a look into God's throne room in heaven and see if it's something worth hoping for.

1. *Describe your mental picture of heaven. How attractive does it seem to you?*

_____

_____

_____

_____

EXPERIENCE IT

"Seek My Face, and you will find all that you have longed for. The deepest yearnings of your heart are for intimacy with Me. I know, because I designed you to desire Me. Do not feel guilty about taking time to be still in My Presence. You are simply responding to the tugs of divinity within you. I made you in My image, and I hid heaven in your heart.

Your yearning for Me is a form of homesickness: longing for your true home in heaven. Do not be afraid to be different from other people. The path I have called you to travel is exquisitely right for you. The more closely you follow My leading, the more fully I can develop your gifts. To follow Me wholeheartedly, you must relinquish your desire to please other people. However, your closeness to Me will bless others by enabling you to shine brightly in this dark world."

—FROM *JESUS CALLING*, JULY 20

2. *What does it mean to have heaven hidden in your heart? Have you experienced that? If so, how?*

_____

_____

_____

_____

_____

3. *Are you aware of homesickness, or yearning for Jesus and your true home in heaven? If so, what is that like for you? Or are your yearnings more about other things? What other things?*

_____

_____

_____

_____

_____

"I want you to know how safe and secure you are in My Presence. That is a fact, totally independent of your feelings. You are on your way to heaven; nothing can prevent you from reaching that destination. There you will see Me face to Face, and your Joy will be off the charts by any earthly standards. Even now, you are never separated from Me, though you must see Me through eyes of faith. I will walk with you till the end of time, and onward into eternity. Although My Presence is a guaranteed promise, that does not necessarily change your feelings. When you forget I am with you, you may experience loneliness or fear. It is through awareness of My Presence that Peace displaces negative feelings. Practice the discipline of walking consciously with Me through each day."

—FROM *JESUS CALLING*, MAY 19

4. *Why is it important to know nothing can prevent followers of Christ from reaching their destination in heaven and seeing God face to Face? How does knowing that help you here and now?*

---

5. *How does walking consciously with Jesus throughout the day strengthen your hope?*

STUDY IT

Read aloud the following passage from Revelation 4:2–11 and 5:11–14. In these verses, the apostle John attempts to describe a vision of heaven he has been given. As you read, note that the living creatures represent a form of angelic beings, and the twenty-four elders symbolize the leaders of God's people (twelve patriarchs of the Old Testament and twelve apostles of the New Testament). The Lamb who was slain is Jesus, who sacrificed His life as an offering on our behalf.

I was in the Spirit, and there before me was a throne in heaven with someone sitting on it. And the one who sat there had the appearance of jasper and ruby. A rainbow that shone like an emerald encircled the throne. Surrounding the throne were twenty-four other thrones, and seated on them were twenty-four elders. They were dressed in white and had crowns of gold on their heads. From the throne came flashes of lightning, rumblings and peals of thunder. In front of the throne, seven lamps were blazing. These are the seven spirits of God. Also in front of the throne there was what looked like a sea of glass, clear as crystal.

In the center, around the throne, were four living creatures, and they were covered with eyes, in front and in back. The first living creature was like a lion, the second was like an ox, the third had a face like a man, the fourth was like a flying eagle. Each of the four living creatures had six wings and was covered with eyes all around, even under its wings. Day and night they never stop saying: "'Holy, holy, holy is the Lord God Almighty,' who was, and is, and is to come."

Whenever the living creatures give glory, honor and thanks to him who sits on the throne and who lives for ever and ever, the twenty-four elders fall down before him who sits on the throne and worship him who lives for ever and ever. They lay their crowns before the throne and say: "You are worthy, our Lord and God, to receive glory and honor and power, for you created all things, and by your will they were created and have their being." . . .

Then I looked and heard the voice of many angels, numbering thousands upon thousands, and ten thousand times ten thousand. They encircled the throne and the living creatures and the elders. In a loud voice they were saying: "Worthy is the Lamb, who was slain, to receive power and wealth and wisdom and strength and honor and glory and praise!"

Then I heard every creature in heaven and on earth and under the earth and on the sea, and all that is in them, saying: "To him who sits on the throne and to the Lamb be praise and honor and glory and power, for ever and ever!"

The four living creatures said, "Amen," and the elders fell down and worshiped.

6. *John can't quite describe what the One on the throne looks like. The best he can do is say He "had the appearance of jasper [a gemstone that comes in a variety of colors] and ruby." What mental picture do you get from John's description of God? Why do you suppose he describes God in terms of gemstones?*

7. *Why would "flashes of lightning, rumblings and peals of thunder" be part of this vision of God's throne room? What do they convey about God's Presence?*

8. *Notice the four living creatures never stop proclaiming God is "holy, holy, holy." Not just a* little *holy, but a* lot *holy. The word* holy *means to be set apart, wholly other, and morally pure. How is it possible for us to be in the Presence of a God who is holy, holy, holy?*

9. *Why do you think worship is such a central activity of heaven? What are the implications for believers here and now?*

10. *What is your overall response to this picture of God's Presence? Are you drawn to it with longing, or does it make you want to step back in reverence and holy fear? Why?*

11. *Read the passage aloud again. Take two minutes of silence to reread the passage, looking for a sentence, phrase, or even one word that stands out as something Jesus wants you to hear. Ask Him to help you hear Him. If you're meeting with a group, the leader will keep track of time. At the end of two minutes, you may share with the group the word or phrase that came to you in the silence.*

12. *Read the passage aloud again. Take two minutes of silence, asking Jesus what He is saying to you through the word or phrase you selected and whether He would like you to do anything in response. If you're meeting with a group, the leader will again keep track of time. At the end of two minutes, you may share with the group what came to you in the silence if you wish.*

13. *If you're meeting with a group, how can the members pray for you? If you're using this study on your own, what would you like to say to God right now?*

_____

_____

_____

_____

LIVE IT

The theme of this week's daily passages is how our future in heaven is relevant to us now. Read each passage slowly, pausing to think about what is being said. Rather than approaching this as an assignment to complete, think of it as an opportunity to meet with a Person. Use any of the questions that are helpful.

Day 1

Read 1 Peter 1:3–5. For what does Peter praise God here?

_____

_____

_____

_____

What is the reason for our living hope? What do we hope for?

How would you describe the inheritance kept in heaven for you? What are you going to inherit?

Until you receive your inheritance in heaven, you are shielded by God's power through faith. Shielded from what? How does that strengthen your hope?

Thank God for the living hope He has given you.

Day 2

Read 1 Peter 1:6–7. Peter begins by saying, "In all this you greatly rejoice," referring to what he mentioned in verses 3–5. How greatly do you rejoice in Jesus' resurrection? Why?

Is Jesus resurrection a long-ago abstraction or something real to you that you think about?

How greatly do you rejoice in your coming inheritance? Is it the faraway future or something that buoys you up here and now?

What reasons for present trials does Peter give? Do his words encourage you to have joy despite your trials? Why or why not?

Spend some time rejoicing in what God has done for you and will do for you.

Day 3

Read 1 Peter 1:8–9. What should be your attitude toward Jesus even though you haven't yet seen Him?

How is it possible to love and believe in someone you've never seen?

Does the salvation of your soul cause you joy, or do you tend to take it for granted?

Take some time to rest in Jesus' Presence, rejoicing in Him for what He has already done for you and what He is going to do.

Day 4

Read Hebrews 6:10–12. What does the author want us to do while we wait for our hope to be fully realized?

Note that when the author speaks of laziness in verse 12, he isn't talking about physical laziness (unwillingness to work) but about spiritual laziness (unwillingness to care about growth in things such as love, hope, and patience). Do you ever struggle with that kind of laziness, where spiritual growth doesn't seem worth the effort? Explain.

Does busyness with other things tend to crowd out your time to devote to growth in love? If so, what are the consequences?

How does hope help you overcome spiritual laziness?

Talk with God honestly about the realities of your life and the time you have to devote to the cultivation of your soul.

Day 5

Read Hebrews 6:19. The author describes hope as "an anchor for the soul, firm and secure." How is hope an anchor for the soul?

What does an anchor do? What happens to a soul without the anchor of hope?

Why should you be confident that what you hope for is firm and secure?

Take some time to meditate on that image of an anchor. How anchored is your soul? What is the evidence? Ask God to more deeply anchor you with secure hope.

OUR HOPE IS IN
GOD'S ABUNDANCE

CONSIDER IT

In the previous session, we saw that worship is at the heart of heaven's business. We can enter into our hope of heaven now by entering deeply into worship. Even if our circumstances don't change, our experience of life now can be richer if we choose to praise and glorify God as a foretaste of heaven.

The Bible offers other pictures of heaven besides a worship service. In this session, we'll see how heaven is also like a banquet. Regardless of our circumstances, we can fix our hope on enjoying that banquet, and God will give us foretastes of that celebration in this life.

1. *When you were a child, what special meals did you have at family celebrations? Give a few examples.*

EXPERIENCE IT

"You are My beloved child. *I chose you before the foundation of the world*, to walk with Me along paths designed uniquely for you. Concentrate on keeping in step with Me, instead of trying to anticipate My plans for you. If you trust that My plans are *to prosper you and not to harm you*, you can relax and enjoy the present moment. Your hope and your future are rooted in heaven, where eternal ecstasy awaits you. Nothing can rob you of your inheritance of unimaginable riches and well-being. Sometimes I grant you glimpses of your glorious future, to encourage you and spur you on. But your main focus should be staying close to Me. I set the pace in keeping with your needs and My purposes."

—FROM *JESUS CALLING*, JUNE 18

2. *What encourages you to trust that God's plans are to prosper you and not to harm you? What, if anything, gets in the way?*

3. *In order to get glimpses of your glorious future, you need to stay close to Jesus. How do you go about doing that?*

"As you sit quietly in My Presence, remember that I am a God of abundance. I will never run out of resources; My capacity to bless you is unlimited. You live in a world of supply and demand, where necessary things are often scarce. Even if you personally have enough, you see poverty in the world around you. It is impossible for you to comprehend the lavishness of My provisions: the fullness of My *glorious riches.* Through spending time in My Presence, you gain glimpses of My overflowing vastness. These glimpses are tiny foretastes of what you will experience eternally in heaven. Even now you have access to as much of Me as you have faith to receive. Rejoice in My abundance—*living by faith, not by sight.*"

—FROM *JESUS CALLING*, MAY 17

4. *What does it mean to say that God is a God of abundance? How does He display His abundance?*

5. *How do we live our lives differently if we see Him as a God of abundance versus seeing our lives as mired in scarcity? Give some examples.*

STUDY IT

Read aloud the following passage from Isaiah 25:6–9. In these verses the prophet Isaiah is foreseeing the ultimate destiny for the mountaintop city of Jerusalem, where he lived. There were many problems in his city, but God revealed that one day a heavenly Jerusalem would fulfill the city's true purpose. The heavenly Jerusalem is our destiny.

> On this mountain the LORD Almighty will prepare
> a feast of rich food for all peoples,
> a banquet of aged wine—
> the best of meats and the finest of wines.
> On this mountain he will destroy
> the shroud that enfolds all peoples,

the sheet that covers all nations;
> he will swallow up death forever.
The Sovereign LORD will wipe away the tears
> from all faces;
he will remove his people's disgrace
> from all the earth.
>> The LORD has spoken.
In that day they will say,
> "Surely this is our God;
>> we trusted in him, and he saved us.
> This is the LORD, we trusted in him;
>> let us rejoice and be glad in his salvation."

6. *Make a mental picture of a banquet filled with rich food and aged wine. What is God saying about heaven when He describes it in these terms? What might the rich food and aged wine symbolize about heaven?*

7. *God says the banquet will be for **all peoples**. Picture a banquet with people from all parts of the world. Why is this an important part of the heavenly banquet?*

8. *The food isn't the best part of a banquet like this. Rather, the best part is that it's a celebration with other people, with Jesus as the Host. Who are some of the people you look forward to seeing at this banquet? What might they be doing? What might Jesus be doing?*

9. *God says He will "swallow up death forever." It will no longer be like a shroud that covers whole nations. In what way is death like a sheet covering us today?*

10. *Praise of the Host will be part of the banquet celebration. Why do the words of praise at the end of the passage repeat the phrase, "We trusted in him"? What role does trust in God play in our preparation for this hoped-for banquet?*

11. *Read the passage aloud again. Take two minutes of silence to reread the passage, looking for a sentence, phrase, or even one word that stands out as something Jesus wants you to hear. Ask Him to help you hear Him. If you're meeting with a group, the leader will keep track of time. At the end of two minutes, you may share your word or phrase with the group if you wish.*

12. *Read the passage aloud again. Take two minutes of silence, asking Jesus what He is saying to you through the word or phrase you selected and whether He would like you to do anything in response. If you're meeting with a group, the leader will again keep track of time. At the end of two minutes, you may share with the group what came to you in the silence if you wish.*

13. *If you're meeting with a group, how can the members pray for you? If you're using this study on your own, what would you like to say to God right now?*

LIVE IT

The theme of this week's daily passages is the heavenly banquet. Read each passage slowly, pausing to think about what is being said. Rather than approaching this as an assignment to complete, think of it as an opportunity to meet with a Person. Use any of the questions that are helpful.

Day 1

Read Luke 14:15–20. What excuses do the people make for turning down the invitation to the banquet?

What excuses do people make today for declining God's invitation to join Him at the celebration feast in heaven?

What excuses, if any, do you struggle with? Why do these excuses often seem so convincing?

Talk with God about the excuses that tempt you. Take some time to thank Him for His invitation to you.

Day 2

Read Luke 14:21–24. How does the master hosting the banquet deal with the excuses?

Why should we be surprised—even shocked—by his orders?

Can you identify in any way with the poor, the crippled, the blind, and the lame? If so, how?

How does your invitation to the banquet make you feel?

How do you deal with other poor, blind, and lame people who are invited? Do you wish they were more "normal"? Why or why not?

Thank God for the people He is bringing into His banquet.

Day 3

Read Psalm 36:7–9. When the psalmist says, "They feast on the abundance of your house," what does he mean? What is the abundance God provides?

Are you feasting? Do you experience abundance, a fountain of life from God, or does your life feel more like scarcity? Explain.

How can you connect with God's abundance? Where does His unfailing love fit in?

Praise God for all He provides—get as specific as you can about what you're grateful for—and ask Him to help you see abundance instead of scarcity in your world.

Day 4

Read John 6:27–29. Why does Jesus say, "Do not work for food that spoils"? Don't we need food?

What is "food that endures for eternal life"? Why is it more important than physical food?

What does it mean to believe in Jesus? What does it involve besides believing information about Him?

_____

_____

_____

_____

Why does Jesus call this the work of God? How does robustly believing in Jesus provide food that endures?

_____

_____

_____

_____

Ask Jesus to help you believe in Him more wholeheartedly and to uproot any areas of unbelief that are cutting you off from His abundance.

Day 5

Read John 6:35, 48–52. What does it mean to call Jesus the "bread of life"?

_____

_____

_____

_____

How does this "bread" keep a person from dying?

Do you tend to be more focused on your physical needs or your spiritual needs? Why is that the case?

Does God care about your physical needs? How do you know?

Why does Jesus place so much emphasis on the need for spiritual food?

Talk with God about your physical needs and your spiritual hunger.

OUR HOPE IS IN GOD'S ETERNAL PROMISES

CONSIDER IT

Sometimes it seems as if our tears, mourning, and pain will never end. We feel hopeless because we see no light at the end of the tunnel. But God promises that those painful things are not forever. We earnestly desire and pray they will not overwhelm us in this life, but even if things are painful now, we can be confident of a day when all tears will be wiped from our eyes. This promise, along with God's promise to be present with us now and to give us foretastes of that future, will strengthen us with hope and joy.

In this session we will spend some more time in the book of Revelation, soaking in a vision of the future God has promised us.

1. *Name three things about your current life that you are grateful for.*

_____

_____

_____

_____

EXPERIENCE IT

"Be still in the Light of My Presence, while I communicate Love to you. There is no force in the universe as powerful as My Love. You are constantly aware of limitations: your own and others'. But there is no limit to My Love; it fills all of space, time, and eternity. *Now you see through a glass, darkly, but someday you will see Me face to Face.* Then you will be able to experience fully *how wide and long and high and deep is My Love for you.* If you were to experience that now, you would be overwhelmed to the point of feeling crushed. But you have an eternity ahead of you, absolutely guaranteed, during which you can enjoy My Presence in unrestricted ecstasy. For now, the knowledge of My loving Presence is sufficient to carry you through each day."

—FROM *JESUS CALLING*, FEBRUARY 24

2. *What can God's people be sure of about the eternity that lies ahead? How does knowing that affect you?*

_____

_____

_____

3. *How can you experience some of that promise here and now? To what extent does this present experience give you hope? Why?*

_____

_____

_____

"Heaven is both present and future. As you walk along your life-path holding My hand, you are already in touch with the essence of heaven: nearness to Me. You can also find many hints of heaven along your pathway, because the earth is radiantly alive with My Presence. Shimmering sunshine awakens your heart, gently reminding you of My brilliant Light. Birds and flowers, trees and skies evoke praises to My holy Name. Keep your eyes and ears fully open as you journey with Me. At the end of your life-path is an entrance to heaven. Only I know when you will reach that destination, but I am preparing you for it each step of the way. The absolute certainty of your heavenly home gives you Peace and Joy, to help you along your journey. You know that you will reach your home in My perfect timing: not one moment too soon or too late. Let the hope of heaven encourage you, as you walk along the path of Life with Me."

—From *Jesus Calling*, April 14

4. *What hints of heaven have you seen in the past few days? If you can't think of any, why do you suppose that's the case?*

_____

_____

_____

_____

5. *What does it mean, in practical terms, to "walk along your life-path holding [Jesus'] hand"? How does a person do that?*

_____

_____

_____

_____

STUDY IT

Read aloud the following passages from Revelation 21:1–5, 9–12, and 18–27. In these verses the apostle John describes His vision of the heavenly Jerusalem coming to a renewed earth. In his day, the countryside was a place of hard work and the wilderness was a place of danger, not recreation. So it made sense for John to describe our hoped-for home in terms of a city full of people, safe and beautiful.

> Then I saw "a new heaven and a new earth," for the first heaven and the first earth had passed away, and there was no longer any sea. I saw the

Holy City, the new Jerusalem, coming down out of heaven from God, prepared as a bride beautifully dressed for her husband. And I heard a loud voice from the throne saying, "Look! God's dwelling place is now among the people, and he will dwell with them. They will be his people, and God himself will be with them and be their God. 'He will wipe every tear from their eyes. There will be no more death' or mourning or crying or pain, for the old order of things has passed away."

He who was seated on the throne said, "I am making everything new!" Then he said, "Write this down, for these words are trustworthy and true." . . .

One of the seven angels who had the seven bowls full of the seven last plagues came and said to me, "Come, I will show you the bride, the wife of the Lamb." And he carried me away in the Spirit to a mountain great and high, and showed me the Holy City, Jerusalem, coming down out of heaven from God. It shone with the glory of God, and its brilliance was like that of a very precious jewel, like a jasper, clear as crystal. It had a great, high wall with twelve gates, and with twelve angels at the gates. On the gates were written the names of the twelve tribes of Israel . . .

The wall was made of jasper, and the city of pure gold, as pure as glass. The foundations of the city walls were decorated with every kind of precious stone. The first foundation was jasper, the second sapphire, the third agate, the fourth emerald, the fifth onyx, the sixth ruby, the seventh chrysolite, the eighth beryl, the ninth topaz, the tenth turquoise, the eleventh jacinth, and the twelfth amethyst. The twelve gates were twelve pearls, each gate made of a single pearl. The great street of the city was of gold, as pure as transparent glass.

I did not see a temple in the city, because the Lord God Almighty and the Lamb are its temple. The city does not need the sun or the moon to shine on it, for the glory of God gives it light, and the Lamb is its lamp. The nations will walk by its light, and the kings of the earth will bring their splendor into it. On no day will its gates ever be shut, for there will be no night there. The glory and honor of the nations will be brought into it. Nothing impure will ever enter it, nor will anyone who does what is shameful or deceitful, but only those whose names are written in the Lamb's book of life.

6. *John tells us God will dwell in the midst of His people in the new Jerusalem, with no distance. Why is that to be greatly hoped for?*

7. *How does it affect you to think about a time when tears, mourning, and pain are permanently over?*

8. *John describes the city's beauty in terms of gold and gemstones. What does that description convey about it? What emotions or thoughts does the description bring up for you?*

9. *The Holy City will be a place where God's people live not just with God but also with each other. What are some of the current challenges of living close to other people that we won't have to worry about in the Holy City?*

10. *How do you think this vision of the Holy City is supposed to affect the way we live now? Does it affect your view of your current circumstances in any ways?*

11. *Read the passage aloud again. Take two minutes of silence to reread the passage, looking for a sentence, phrase, or even one word that stands out as something Jesus wants you to hear. Ask Him to help you hear Him. If you're meeting with a group, the leader will keep track of time. At the end of two minutes, you may share your word or phrase with the group if you wish.*

12. *Read the passage aloud again. Take two minutes of silence, asking Jesus what He is saying to you through the word or phrase you selected and whether He would like you to do anything in response. If you're meeting with a group, the leader will again keep track of time. At the end of two minutes, you may share with the group what came to you in the silence if you wish.*

13. *If you're meeting with a group, how can the members pray for you? If you're using this study on your own, what would you like to say to God right now?*

LIVE IT

The theme of this week's readings is connecting our hope with our daily lives. Read each passage slowly, pausing to think about what is being said. Rather than approaching this as an assignment to complete, think of it as an opportunity to meet with a Person. Use any of the questions that are helpful.

Day 1

Read Ephesians 1:15–18. What does Paul ask God to do for his readers?

Have you ever prayed for the Spirit of wisdom and revelation to help you know God better? Try doing that now. Why do you need the eyes of your heart enlightened? What is your heart like without this?

What have you learned so far in this study about the hope to which God has called you?

What thoughts and feelings have you been having about that hope?

_____

_____

_____

_____

Talk with God about the hope you feel and how that affects the way you deal with current circumstances. Ask Him for wisdom and revelation.

Day 2

Read Ephesians 1:19–23. This is the continuation of Paul's prayer in verse 18. What does Paul pray for his readers here?

_____

_____

_____

_____

How has God displayed His power? Does that impress you? Why or why not?

_____

_____

_____

_____

What difference does it make that God has placed all things under Jesus' feet?

What are the powers and authorities that currently affect your life? Do you believe Jesus is far above those? Why or why not?

Ask God to enlighten the eyes of your heart so you can see Jesus above any other powers in your life.

Day 3

Read 1 Timothy 6:17–19. What are the signs that we have put our hope in wealth? Why is it foolish to put our hope there?

How has God richly provided us with things to enjoy?

How can we be rich in good deeds?

What is "the life that is truly life"? What other kinds of life do people run after that aren't truly life?

Look for one way to lay up real treasure for yourself today. Ask God to show you how.

Day 4

Read Hebrews 10:22–25. Does faith give you full assurance, or do you struggle with doubts? Explain.

If you have doubts, would talking about them to some trusted person help you? Why or why not?

According to this reading, why can you hold unswervingly to your hope?

What does the writer urge you to do in your relationships with others? How can you do that this week?

Who encourages you? Who can you encourage? Ask God to put some-one's name on your heart.

Day 5

Read Psalm 25:1–5. What does it mean to be put to shame?

When have you seen someone put to shame or been put to shame yourself?

Why are you safe from that if you hope in God? Are you able to trust that promise?

What does it mean to put your hope in God all day long? How would that make a difference in your life?

Pray this psalm back to the Lord, adding in things about your own circumstances.

OUR HOPE IS
IN THE EARTH'S
TRANSFORMATION

CONSIDER IT

Have you ever been to the desert? If not, it's hard to imagine how baking hot and dry it is there. Your nose and mouth dry out. The wind stings your eyes. The sun is so strong that despite the heat you want to cover your skin to protect it. Without sunglasses and a hat, the glare is unbearable.

There are various forms of deserts all over the Middle East, so it was a familiar landscape to the biblical writers. The desert had strong associations for them. When God spoke through the prophet Isaiah and said He was going to transform the desert, Isaiah's hearers knew exactly how significant that was. In this session we will consider what that promise means for us.

1. *When you think of the desert, what images or memories come to mind?*

_____

_____

_____

_____

EXPERIENCE IT

"Remember that you live in a fallen world: an abnormal world tainted by sin. Much frustration and failure result from your seeking perfection in this life. There is nothing perfect in this world except Me. That is why closeness to Me satisfies deep yearnings and fills you with Joy. I have planted longing for perfection in every human heart. This is a good desire, which I alone can fulfill. But most people seek this fulfillment in other people and earthly pleasures or achievements. Thus they create idols, before which they bow down. *I will have no other gods before Me!* Make Me the deepest desire of your heart. Let Me fulfill your yearning for perfection."

—FROM *JESUS CALLING*, JUNE 5

2. *Give an example of how seeking perfection in this life can lead to frustration and failure.*

_____

_____

_____

_____

3. *How could making Jesus the deepest desire of your heart help you?*

_____

_____

_____

4. *What can you do to cultivate that desire?*

_____

_____

_____

_____

"Hope is a golden cord connecting you to heaven. This cord helps you hold your head up high, even when multiple trials are buffeting you. I never leave your side, and I never let go of your hand. But without the cord of hope, your head may slump and your feet may shuffle as you journey uphill with Me. Hope lifts your perspective from your weary feet to the glorious view you can see from the high road. You are reminded that the road we're traveling together is ultimately a highway to heaven. When you consider this radiant destination, the roughness or smoothness of the road ahead becomes much less significant. I am training you to hold in your heart a dual focus: My continual Presence and the hope of heaven."

—FROM *JESUS CALLING*, JULY 27

5. *As you have done this study, has considering your radiant destination in heaven made the roughness or smoothness of your road seem less significant? Describe what is changing you.*

_____

_____

_____

6. *What do you think helps a person become gripped by the hope of heaven? How can a person who is struggling with a rough road grow in hope?*

_____

_____

_____

STUDY IT

Read aloud the following passages from Isaiah 35:1–2, 5–10. In these verses the prophet Isaiah uses poetry to evoke a picture of life after Christ returns. As you read, note that in Isaiah's day the desert was a dangerous place that barely supported life and was populated with animals (such as jackals) that could harm people. By contrast, Lebanon, Carmel, and Sharon were some of the most lush and beautiful places in his part of the world. Papyrus was a plant that grew in wetlands, not in a dry desert. "Zion" was the name of the mountain on which Jerusalem was built, so it is effectively a name for the restored Jerusalem we have seen in earlier Scripture passages.

> The desert and the parched land will be glad;
>> the wilderness will rejoice and blossom.
> Like the crocus, it will burst into bloom;
>> it will rejoice greatly and shout for joy.
> The glory of Lebanon will be given to it,
>> the splendor of Carmel and Sharon;
> they will see the glory of the LORD,
>> the splendor of our God . . .
> Then will the eyes of the blind be opened
>> and the ears of the deaf unstopped.
> Then will the lame leap like a deer,
>> and the mute tongue shout for joy.
> Water will gush forth in the wilderness
>> and streams in the desert.
> The burning sand will become a pool,
>> the thirsty ground bubbling springs.
> In the haunts where jackals once lay,
>> grass and reeds and papyrus will grow.
> And a highway will be there;
>> it will be called the Way of Holiness;
>> it will be for those who walk on that Way.
> The unclean will not journey on it;
>> wicked fools will not go about on it.

No lion will be there,
    nor any ravenous beast;
    they will not be found there.
But only the redeemed will walk there,
    and those the LORD has rescued will return.
They will enter Zion with singing;
    everlasting joy will crown their heads.
Gladness and joy will overtake them,
    and sorrow and sighing will flee away.

7. *What might it mean to say the desert will shout for joy? How can a desert shout?*

_____

_____

_____

_____

8. *The glory of the Lord is His magnificent Presence. What do you learn about God's glory when Isaiah compares it to the lush landscape of Lebanon, which was heavily forested with cedars in his day?*

_____

_____

_____

_____

9. *Not only will the desert be transformed, but disabled people (the blind, the lame, the deaf) will be transformed as well. What transformations in the world or in particular people's lives do you most look forward to?*

10. *What does Isaiah say about the highway? What is it for? Who will and will not use it?*

11. *Read the passage aloud again. Take two minutes of silence to reread the passage, looking for a sentence, phrase, or even one word that stands out as something Jesus wants you to hear. Ask Him to help you hear Him. If you're meeting with a group, the leader will keep track of time. At the end of two minutes, you may share your word or phrase with the group if you wish.*

12. *Read the passage aloud again. Take two minutes of silence, asking Jesus what He is saying to you through the word or phrase you selected and whether He would like you to do anything in response. If you're meeting with a group, the leader will again keep track of time. At the end of two minutes, you may share with the group what came to you in the silence if you wish.*

13. *If you're meeting with a group, how can the members pray for you? If you're using this study on your own, what would you like to say to God right now?*

LIVE IT

This week's Scripture readings deal with more pictures of hope from Isaiah. Read each passage slowly, pausing to think about what is being said. Rather than approaching this as an assignment to complete, think of it as an opportunity to meet with a Person. Use any of the questions that are helpful.

Day 1

Read Isaiah 35:3–4. These verses come from the middle of the passage you read with your group. What effect should Isaiah's vision of hope have on you?

What do you think it means to "strengthen the feeble hands" and "steady the knees"? How do you go about doing that?

Does it help you to know that God will come to save you eventually, even if that is years from now?

What do you long for Him to do for you right now?

_____

_____

_____

_____

Pour out your heart and express the hope you have in Him.

Day 2

Read Isaiah 11:3–5. These words refer to Christ when He comes as King to rule. What can we expect Him to do?

_____

_____

_____

_____

What does this passage say about God's justice and righteousness?

_____

_____

_____

_____

What longings does it stir in you when you read about what Christ will do when He returns to rule?

Offer Christ a prayer to act with justice and faithfulness in your world. Thank Him that ultimately justice will prevail, no matter what happens here and now.

Day 3

Read Isaiah 11:6–9. In this passage Isaiah continues to talk about Christ's kingdom. Do you think his words are literal, or are they poetic language for relationships among people?

How do his words affect you? Why does "knowledge of the Lord" have such a strong effect on violent creatures?

Where would you like to see the knowledge of the Lord spread today?

Offer God a prayer asking that the knowledge of Him would be spread to the world.

Day 4

Read Isaiah 32:1–5. What does Isaiah say about government when Christ returns as King?

How important is good government to you? Is that something you long for, or is it not so high on the list of things you are concerned about?

If you live in peace and safety, offer God a prayer of thanks for that fact. How easy is it for you to imagine rulers who are like shelter from the wind? What would make them that way?

What do you think "the fearful heart will know and understand" when Christ returns to reign?

Talk with God about justice and tell Him any longings you have about it.

Day 5

Read Isaiah 49:14–16. Are you ever tempted to think, "The Lord has forsaken me"? If so, why?

What assurances does this passage give if you feel that way? How do these assurances affect you? Which statement touches you most deeply?

Think about the palms of Jesus' hands with wounds from being nailed to the cross. How is that like having your name engraved on His hands?

Offer Jesus a prayer of thanks for His sacrifice. Tell Him what you long for Him to do, and pray with trust in His care.

OUR HOPE IS IN THE RESURRECTION

CONSIDER IT

Many religions teach the immortality of the soul—the idea that humans continue to exist beyond death as disembodied souls. However, Christianity doesn't simply teach that souls are immortal. It affirms that, just as Jesus was raised bodily from the dead into a glorified body, someday our souls will in some fashion be reclothed with bodies that are recognizably ours. This resurrection is not reincarnation—it will happen once, when heaven and earth are renewed at the end of this age. Further, we won't regain *mortal bodies* to live in this *broken world* but *renewed bodies* to live in a *renewed world*. Our hope, therefore, has a bodily dimension. In this session, we'll think about the implications of this hope.

1. *It's easy to think of things we don't like about our bodies (they're very imperfect now). So instead, name three things about your body that you're grateful for.*

EXPERIENCE IT

"Do not long for the absence of problems in your life. That is an unrealistic goal, since *in this world you will have trouble.* You have an eternity of problem-free living reserved for you in heaven. Rejoice in that inheritance, which no one can take away from you, but do not seek your heaven on earth. Begin each day anticipating problems, asking Me to equip you for whatever difficulties you will encounter. The best equipping is My living Presence, *My hand that never lets go of yours.* Discuss everything with Me. Take a lighthearted view of trouble, seeing it as a challenge that you and I together can handle. Remember that I am on your side, and *I have overcome the world.*"

—FROM *JESUS CALLING*, MAY 8

2. *How can it help you to begin each day by asking God to equip you with His living Presence? How can it help you to begin each day by discussing your problems with Him? What practical aid does that give?*

3. *Do you believe you and God together can handle whatever trouble comes into your life? What is the evidence?*

"I love you with an everlasting Love, which flows out from the depths of eternity. Before you were born, I knew you. Ponder the awesome mystery of a Love that encompasses you from before birth to beyond the grave. Modern man has lost the perspective of eternity. To distract himself from the gaping jaws of death, he engages in ceaseless activity and amusement. The practice of being still in My Presence is almost a lost art, yet it is this very stillness that enables you to experience My eternal Love. You need the certainty of My loving Presence in order to weather the storms of life. During times of severe testing, even the best theology can fail you if it isn't accompanied by experiential knowledge of Me. The ultimate protection against sinking during life's storms is devoting time to develop your friendship with Me."

—FROM *JESUS CALLING*, DECEMBER 1

4. *Do you agree that we use ceaseless activity and amusement to distract ourselves from the fear of death? If so, what should you do about that? If not, why aren't you convinced?*

---

5. *We need the certainty of God's loving Presence to have solid hope in the midst of life's storms. How do you cultivate that certainty? How are you doing at cultivating it? What help, if any, do you need?*

Study It

Read aloud the following passages from 1 Corinthians 15:35, 42–44, 50–54. Here, the apostle Paul speaks about the bodily resurrection of Christians who have died, as well as the bodily transformation of Christians who have not yet died when Christ comes for us. He speaks of bodies being "sown" like seeds when they are buried in the earth.

> But someone will ask, "How are the dead raised? With what kind of body will they come?" . . .
>
> The body that is sown is perishable, it is raised imperishable; it is sown in dishonor, it is raised in glory; it is sown in weakness, it is raised in power; it is sown a natural body, it is raised a spiritual body . . .
>
> I declare to you, brothers and sisters, that flesh and blood cannot inherit the kingdom of God, nor does the perishable inherit the imperishable. Listen, I tell you a mystery: We will not all sleep, but we will all be changed—in a flash, in the twinkling of an eye, at the last trumpet. For the trumpet will sound, the dead will be raised imperishable, and we will be changed. For the perishable must clothe itself with the imperishable, and the mortal with immortality. When the perishable has been clothed with the imperishable, and the mortal with immortality, then the saying that is written will come true: "Death has been swallowed up in victory."

6. *What does Paul tell us in this passage about the bodies we will have when we are raised from the dead?*

7. *When Paul speaks of a "spiritual" body, he doesn't mean a ghostly, insubstantial body. He means a body animated by the Holy Spirit, not just by biological mechanisms. Our bodies will be more than natural (supernatural), not less than natural. What might be some things that spiritual bodies can do that natural bodies can't?*

8. *Why do you think Paul so strongly emphasizes the defeat of death? How does Christ's defeat of death release Christians from the burden of death that the world lives with?*

9. *How do you think the hope of resurrection should affect believers' attitudes toward death in the here and now?*

10. *How should our hope of resurrection affect our attitude toward aging and physical disability?*

---

11. *Read the passage aloud again. Take two minutes of silence to reread the passage, looking for a sentence, phrase, or even one word that stands out as something Jesus wants you to hear. Ask Him to help you hear Him. If you're meeting with a group, the leader will keep track of time. At the end of two minutes, you may share your word or phrase with the group if you wish.*

---

12. *Read the passage aloud again. Take two minutes of silence, asking Jesus what He is saying to you through the word or phrase you selected and whether He would like you to do anything in response. If you're meeting with a group, the leader will again keep track of time. At the end of two minutes, you may share with the group what came to you in the silence if you wish.*

---

13. *If you're meeting with a group, how can the members pray for you? If you're using this study on your own, what would you like to say to God right now?*

Live It

This week's readings deal with the theme of resurrection. Read each passage slowly, pausing to think about what is being said. Rather than approaching this as an assignment to complete, think of it as an opportunity to meet with a Person. Use any of the questions that are helpful.

Day 1

Read Philippians 3:20–21. What do you think it means that even while believers are here on earth their citizenship is in heaven?

What are some of the privileges of being a citizen of heaven? What attitude should believers have toward their temporary stay in this world?

Paul says our bodies at present are "lowly." How do you experience the lowliness of your body? What do you think is a good attitude to have toward a lowly body? Should you despise your body because it is not yet glorified?

Talk with God about the way He wants you to view your body.

Day 2

Read Luke 24:36–43. These verses depict a scene in which Jesus appears to His followers after His resurrection. What do you observe about His resurrected body? How was it recognizably a body?

Why do you think Jesus made such a point of convincing His followers that He wasn't a ghost? What might this passage tell you about the resurrected body that you can look forward to?

Why should believers, like the disciples, feel joy and amazement at the hope of one day receiving this resurrected body?

Say a prayer of praise to God for raising Jesus bodily from the dead.

Day 3

Read John 20:19–29. This is another account of Jesus' first meetings with the disciples after His resurrection. How do you think Jesus was able to get to the disciples even though the doors of their room were locked? What does this imply about His resurrected body?

Why do you suppose Jesus still had the wounds of crucifixion in His hands and His side? Why didn't those go away when He was raised from the dead?

What scars might you be pleased to retain when you are raised? What aspects of your lowly body will you be glad to lose?

Say a prayer of praise to Jesus for His wounds and what they represent for you.

Day 4

Read 1 Corinthians 15:17–19. What difference does it make for us that Christ has been raised?

Why does Jesus' resurrection—not just His crucifixion—matter for our salvation?

Why does Jesus' resurrection matter for this life? Why does it matter for the next life?

What does Jesus' resurrection prove about Him?

Praise God for raising Christ from the dead.

Day 5

Read 1 Corinthians 15:55–58. What does Paul mean when he says "the sting of death is sin"? Why is sin no longer a deadly danger if you trust in Christ?

Paul wants your freedom from fear to liberate you to do the Lord's work. Do you feel that liberation? What other related fears still cling to you?

How can the hope of resurrection free you from those fears?

Thank God for removing the sting of death.

OUR HOPE GROWS
IN PERSEVERANCE

CONSIDER IT

Imagine a baseball game in which the team on the field had a slow-throwing pitcher and no players at first, second, or third base. How interesting would it be to watch? Not very. The batters would bang out hits so easily that there would be little suspense. In fact, if the batters knew ahead of time they would be up against such a weak opponent, they probably wouldn't even bother to practice.

No, we like to watch games where the athletes are up against some real challenge. We cheer when they persevere against real odds and overcome them. That's the kind of victory worth hoping for. Easy, lazy victories require little strength and little hope. In this session we'll consider the role that perseverance plays in building our hope muscles and creating victories worth celebrating.

1. *When you were a child, did you tend to stick to activities you knew you were good at or did you try things that required hard work and the risk of failure? Give an example.*

EXPERIENCE IT

"Give up the illusion that you deserve a problem-free life. Part of you is still hungering for the resolution of all difficulties. This is a false hope! As I told My disciples, *in the world you will have trouble.* Link your hope not to problem solving in this life but to the promise of an eternity of problem-free life in heaven. Instead of seeking perfection in this fallen world, pour your energy into seeking Me: the Perfect One. It is possible to enjoy Me and glorify Me in the midst of adverse circumstances. In fact, My Light shines most brightly through believers who trust Me in the dark. That kind of trust is supernatural: a production of

My indwelling Spirit. When things seem all wrong, trust Me anyway. I am much less interested in right circumstances than in right responses to whatever comes your way."

—FROM *JESUS CALLING*, JANUARY 26

2. *How easy is it for you to pour your energy into seeking God rather than a problem-free life? What helps you do that? What gets in the way?*

3. *We don't need to give up all hope of seeing difficulties in this life resolved. It's more a matter of holding those hopes lightly so we don't fall into despair when some difficulty is persistent. Is despair ever a temptation for you? If so, what do you do when it feels tempting?*

"Self-pity is a slimy, bottomless pit. Once you fall in, you tend to go deeper and deeper into the mire. As you slide down those slippery walls, you are well on your way to depression, and the darkness is profound. Your only hope is to look up and see the Light of My Presence shining down on you. Though the Light looks dim from your perspective, deep in the pit, those rays of hope can reach you at any depth. While you focus on Me in trust, you rise ever so slowly out of the abyss of despair. Finally, you can reach up and grasp My hand. I will pull you out into the Light again. I will gently cleanse you, washing off the clinging mire. I will cover you with My righteousness and walk with you down the path of Life."

—FROM *JESUS CALLING*, JULY 16

4. *Why is self-pity such a danger?*

5. *What is the solution to self-pity?*

STUDY IT

Read aloud the following passage from Romans 5:1–5. In these verses, the apostle Paul talks about the process by which we develop hope.

> Therefore, since we have been justified through faith, we have peace with God through our Lord Jesus Christ, through whom we have gained access by faith into this grace in which we now stand. And we boast in the hope of the glory of God. Not only so, but we also glory in our sufferings, because we know that suffering produces perseverance; perseverance, character; and character, hope. And hope does not put us to shame, because God's love has been poured out into our hearts through the Holy Spirit, who has been given to us.

6. *The "hope of the glory of God" is the hope of seeing His magnificent, light-filled Presence face to Face. What does it mean to boast about this? Why would we boast about this hope?*

7. *Why do we glory in our sufferings?*

8. *What is perseverance?*

9. *Suffering doesn't produce perseverance automatically. It can produce bitterness and despair. However, suffering plus God's grace plus our willing cooperation produces perseverance. What attitudes and actions reflect a willingness to cooperate with God?*

10. *Surprisingly perhaps, hope doesn't grow where there is no suffering. It grows out of perseverance in the midst of suffering. What is it about perseverance that fosters the kind of character that leads to hope?*

11. *Read the passage aloud again. Take two minutes of silence to reread the passage, looking for a sentence, phrase, or even one word that stands out as something Jesus wants you to hear. Ask Him to help you hear Him. If you're meeting with a group, the leader will keep track of time. At the end of two minutes, you may share your word or phrase with the group if you wish.*

12. *Read the passage aloud again. Take two minutes of silence, asking Jesus what He is saying to you through the word or phrase you selected and whether He would like you to do anything in response. If you're meeting with a group, the leader will again keep track of time. At the end of two minutes, you may share with the group what came to you in the silence if you wish.*

13. *If you're meeting with a group, how can the members pray for you? If you're using this study on your own, what would you like to say to God right now?*

LIVE IT

This week's readings deal with the theme of perseverance. Read each passage slowly, pausing to think about what is being said. Rather than approaching this as an assignment to complete, think of it as an opportunity to meet with a Person. Use any of the questions that are helpful.

Day 1

Read Titus 2:11–14. What does Paul mean when he says "the grace of God has appeared"? What should be our response to this grace?

How can a self-controlled life be a rich and fulfilling life? How is such a life more rich and fulfilling than one without self-control?

What is our "blessed hope"? Why is doing good an appropriate response to that hope? How does doing good require perseverance?

Thank God for His grace, and praise Him for giving you the blessed hope you are waiting for.

Day 2

Read 2 Thessalonians 1:4–10. Paul writes these words to a group of believers who are being persecuted for their faith in Jesus. Why does he boast about them? How does their perseverance prove that God's judgment is right?

When will God give relief to these believers? Does Paul imply they should be frustrated or despairing if relief doesn't come sooner than that? Why or why not?

Do Paul's words encourage you in any ways? For what do you currently need perseverance?

Cry out to God to strengthen you and talk openly with Him about your problems, knowing He cares deeply about you.

Day 3

Read Hebrews 2:10–11. What does it mean to call Jesus the "pioneer" (NIV), or "founder" (ESV) or "captain" (NKJV), of our salvation?

If Jesus was sinless, in what sense was He made perfect through what He suffered? In what sense are we made perfect through suffering?

While this doesn't make the bad things we suffer any less bad, it does mean God can bring something good (our holiness) out of them. Do you want holiness enough to endure what you are currently enduring? Why or why not?

Talk with God about His process of transforming you into the person you were born to be. Tell Him honestly your thoughts, and thank Him that Jesus is your brother in this process.

Day 4

Read Hebrews 2:17–18. Jesus was fully human in every way. How is that a good thing for you?

_____

_____

_____

How is Jesus a merciful and faithful high priest for you in your current circumstances?

_____

_____

_____

Do you think Jesus was ever tempted to give up hope? Why or why not?

_____

_____

_____

Thank Jesus for His mercy and faithfulness in what you are going through. Thank Him that He was willing to suffer when He was tempted. Ask Him to help you resist the temptation to give up hope. Ask Him to strengthen hope in you, and thank Him for His willingness to do so.

Day 5

Read Hebrews 12:1–3. The writer refers to a cloud of faithful people who have gone before you, testifying that persevering in faith is the right path. What does he urge you to do?

What are the things that hinder you from perseverance or hope?

How did Jesus demonstrate perseverance?

How can you go about fixing your eyes on Jesus? What are some things you should not fix your eyes on?

Praise Jesus for enduring the cross for your sake.

SESSION 8

OUR HOPE LEADS TO STRENGTH

CONSIDER IT

We've talked about the focus of our hope—that guaranteed time in the future when we will see God face to Face, when our bodies will be made like Jesus' glorified body, when we will worship Him with the angels, when we will feast with Him at His banquet. We can cultivate this hope by worshiping God here and now with one another, by spending time in His Presence, by paying attention to His Presence as we go through our days, and by choosing to persevere rather than give up when life is hard.

Where do we get the strength to persevere? From God, of course. In this final session, we'll look at His promise to renew our strength when we place our hope in Him.

1. *What is one specific thing God has revealed to you during this study on receiving Christ's hope? How are you grateful for that?*

EXPERIENCE IT

"Waiting on Me means directing your attention to Me in hopeful anticipation of what I will do. It entails trusting Me with every fiber of your being, instead of trying to figure things out yourself. Waiting on Me is the way I designed you to live: all day, every day. I created you to stay conscious of Me as you go about your daily duties. I have promised many blessings to those who wait on Me: *renewed strength*, living above one's circumstances, resurgence of hope, awareness of My continual Presence. Waiting on Me enables you to glorify Me by living in deep dependence on Me, ready to do My will. It also helps you to enjoy Me; *in My Presence is fullness of Joy.*"

—FROM *JESUS CALLING*, MARCH 26

2. *What does it mean to wait on the Lord? How do you go about doing this in practical terms?*

3. *Choose one of the blessings of waiting on the Lord suggested in this reading. Why is that blessing important to you personally? Are you currently experiencing it? If not, what do you need to do to experience it more?*

"I am the culmination of all your hopes and desires. *I am the Alpha and the Omega, the first and the last: who is and was and is to come.* Before you knew Me, you expressed your longing for Me in hurtful ways. You were ever so vulnerable to the evil around you in the world. But now My Presence safely shields you, enfolding you in My loving arms. *I have lifted you out of darkness into My marvelous Light.* Though I have brought many pleasures into your life, not one of them is essential. Receive My blessings with open hands. Enjoy My good gifts, but do not cling to them. Turn your attention to *the Giver of all good things*, and rest in the knowledge that you are complete in Me. The one thing you absolutely need is the one thing you can never lose: My Presence with you."

—FROM *JESUS CALLING*, OCTOBER 11

4. *Think of one of the major hopes you have. How is God the culmination of that hope?*

5. *What does it mean to cling to one of God's gifts? How do you know if you're clinging to it?*

Study It

Read aloud the following passage from Isaiah 40:27–31. In these verses, the prophet Isaiah addresses the people of Israel (also called Jacob) who are suffering under the difficult circumstances of exile from the Promised Land. His words can be applied to anyone in difficult circumstances.

> Why do you complain, Jacob?
>   Why do you say, Israel,
> "My way is hidden from the LORD;
>   my cause is disregarded by my God"?
> Do you not know?
>   Have you not heard?
> The LORD is the everlasting God,
>   the Creator of the ends of the earth.
> He will not grow tired or weary,
>   and his understanding no one can fathom.

He gives strength to the weary
    and increases the power of the weak.
Even youths grow tired and weary,
    and young men stumble and fall;
but those who hope in the LORD
    will renew their strength.
They will soar on wings like eagles;
    they will run and not grow weary,
    they will walk and not be faint.

6. *Israel complains, "God is disregarding my cause, what I rightly deserve." How does Isaiah argue against that complaint?*

7. *In dealing with your circumstances, does it help you to know the Lord is the Creator of this earth and His understanding is unfathomable? If so, how? If not, why not?*

8. *What does this passage promise to those who place their hope in the Lord?*

9. *In practical terms, what does this kind of hope involve? What do you do to cultivate and practice it?*

10. *Have you ever given in to hopelessness? If so, what was that like? Have you experienced greater strength when you hope in the Lord, as opposed to placing your hope in other things? Describe your experience.*

11. *Read the passage aloud again. Take two minutes of silence to reread the passage, looking for a sentence, phrase, or even one word that stands out as something Jesus wants you to hear. Ask Him to help you hear Him. If you're meeting with a group, the leader will keep track of time. At the end of two minutes, you may share your word or phrase with the group if you wish.*

12. *Read the passage aloud again. Take two minutes of silence, asking Jesus what He is saying to you through the word or phrase you selected and whether He would like you to do anything in response. If you're meeting with a group, the leader will again keep track of time. At the end of two minutes, you may share with the group what came to you in the silence if you wish.*

13. *If you're meeting with a group, how can the members pray for you? If you're using this study on your own, what would you like to say to God right now?*

LIVE IT

This week's readings deal with the theme of cultivating hope in the Lord. Read each passage slowly, pausing to think about what is being said. Rather than approaching this as an assignment to complete, think of it as an opportunity to meet with a Person. Use any of the questions that are helpful.

Day 1

Read Psalm 62:5–8. How does this passage describe God? What does it mean to call Him "my rock"?

What does it mean to "find rest in God" (verse 5, NIV) or "wait silently for God" (NKJV)? What other things might a person be tempted to find rest in?

Why shouldn't we seek our ultimate rest in anything but God? How do other things disappoint us?

Pour out your heart to God, telling Him honestly what you need.

Day 2

Read Psalm 43:3–5. For what does this psalmist ask? How does he deal with the fact that his soul is downcast?

Do you think the psalmist's way of dealing with a downcast soul will work for you? Why or why not?

How can you go to the altar of God and praise Him? What will putting your hope in Him today involve?

Offer God a prayer of praise and hope.

Day 3

Read Psalm 33:16–22. What are some things people are tempted to place their hope in when they are fearful about such things as war or hunger? What are you tempted to place your hope in when you are fearful?

Horses were a vital part of a nation's military when this psalm was written, yet the psalmist calls them "a vain hope" (verse 17). Why is military might ultimately no true source of hope for a nation?

The psalmist says the Lord's caring eyes are on those whose hope is in His "unfailing love" (verse 18). Why should we be confident His love is unfailing?

For what circumstance do you most need to be able to hope in His unfailing love today?

_____

_____

_____

Offer verses 20–22 to God as a prayer.

Day 4

Read Psalm 147:10–14. What pleases the Lord? What are some of the good things He does for those who place their hope in Him?

_____

_____

_____

How has God protected you and satisfied you?

_____

_____

_____

What other needs is God providing for?

_____

_____

_____

Do you tend to focus more on what you don't have? If so, take an inventory of the ways God provides for you. Tell Him what you still need and ask Him to strengthen your hope.

Day 5

Read Psalm 130:5–8. What do you think it means to put your hope in God's word?

Why do watchmen wait fervently for morning?

What reasons does this passage give for putting your hope in the Lord? Do those reasons motivate you? Why or why not?

Look for ways today to cultivate the hope you have in the Lord.

LEADER'S NOTES

Thank you for your willingness to lead a group through this *Jesus Calling* study. The rewards of being a leader are different from the rewards of participating, and we hope you find your own walk with Jesus deepened by this experience. In many ways, your group meeting will be structured like other Bible studies in which you've participated. You'll want to open in prayer, for example, and ask people to silence their phones. These leader's notes will focus on elements of the study that may be new to you.

CONSIDER IT

This first portion of the study functions as an icebreaker. It gets the group members thinking about the topic at hand by asking them to share things from their own experience. Some people may want to tell a long story in response to one of these questions, but the goal is to keep the answers brief. Ideally, you want everyone in the group to have a chance to respond to the *Consider It* questions, so you may want to explain up front that everyone needs to limit his or her answer to one minute.

With the rest of the study, it is generally not a good idea to have everyone answer every question—a free-flowing discussion is more desirable. But with the *Consider It* questions, you can go around the circle. Encourage shy people to share, but don't force them. Tell the group members they should feel free to pass if they prefer not to answer one of these questions.

EXPERIENCE IT

This is the group's chance to talk about excerpts from the *Jesus Calling* devotional. You will need to monitor this discussion closely so that you have enough time for the Bible study. If the group has a long and rich discussion on one of the devotional excerpts, you may choose to skip the other one and move on to the Bible study. Don't feel obliged to cover every question if the discussion is fruitful. On the other hand, do move on if the group starts to ramble or gets off on a tangent.

STUDY IT

Try to do the *Study It* exercise in session 1 on your own before the group meets the first time so you can coach people on what to expect. Note that this section may be a little different from Bible studies your group has done in the past. The group will talk about the Bible passage as usual, but then there will be several minutes of silence so individuals can pray about what God might want to say to them personally through the read-ing. It will be up to you to keep track of the time and call people back to the discussion when the time is up. (There are some good phone apps for timers that play a gentle chime or other pleasant sound instead of a disruptive noise.) If the group members aren't used to being silent in a group, brief them on what to expect.

Don't be afraid to let people sit in silence. Two minutes of this may seem like a long time at first, but it will help to train group members to sit in silence with God when they are alone. They can sit where they are in the circle, or if you have space, you can let them go off alone to another room. As you introduce the exercise, tell them where they are free to go. If your group meets in a home, ask the host before the meeting which rooms are available for use. Some people will be more comfortable in silence if they have a bit of space from others.

When the group gathers back together after the time of silence, invite them to share what they experienced. There are several questions provided in this study guide that you can ask. Note that it's not necessary to cover every question if the group has a good discussion going. Again, it's also not necessary to go around the circle and make everyone share.

Don't be concerned if group members are quiet after the exercise and slow to share. People are often quiet when they are pulling together their ideas, and the exercise will have been a new experience for many of them. Just ask a question and let it hang in the air until someone shares. You can then say, "Thank you. What about others? What came to you when you sat with the passage?"

Some people may say they found it hard to quiet their minds enough to focus on the passage for several minutes. Tell them that's okay. They are practicing a skill, and sometimes skills take time to learn. If they learn to sit quietly with God's Word in a group, they will become much more comfortable sitting with the Word on their own. Remind them that spending time each day in God's Word is one of the most valuable things they can do for their spiritual lives.

PREPARATION

It's not necessary for group members to prepare anything for the study ahead of time. At the end of each study are suggestions for ways they can spend time in God's Word during the next five days of the week. These daily times are optional but valuable, so encourage the group to do them. Also invite them to bring their questions and insights back to the group at your next meeting, especially if they had a breakthrough moment or if they didn't understand something.

As the leader, there are a few things you should do to prepare for each meeting:

- *Read through the session.* This will help you to become familiar with the content and know how to structure the discussion times.

- *Spend five to ten minutes doing the Study It questions on your own.* When the group meets you'll be watching the clock, so you'll probably have a more fulfilling time with the passage if you do the exercise ahead of time. You can then reread the passage again when the group meets. This way, you'll be sure to have the passage even more deeply in your mind than group members do.

- *Pray for your group.* Pray especially that God will guide them into a deeper experience of the hope they have in Jesus.

- *Bring extra supplies to your meeting.* Group members should bring their own pens for writing notes, but it is a good idea to have extras available for those who forget. You may also want to bring paper and additional Bibles for those who forget to bring their study guides.

Below you will find suggested answers for some of the study questions. Note that in many cases there is no one right answer. Answers will vary, especially when the group members are sharing their personal experiences.

Session 1: Our Hope Is Future-Directed

1. *Answers will vary. The goal here is to get people thinking about hope in the biblical sense. The items they name can be mundane (like summer vacation or losing weight) or more spiritually oriented (like heaven and seeing loved ones again).*

2. *At one level, "heaven" here stands for God, who reigns in heaven. Hope connects us to God and gives us access to the good things He wants to give us, especially Himself and His strength to deal with situations on earth. Also, as we'll see, heaven is where our hopes will ultimately be satisfied.*

3. *Among other things, placing our hope in God frees us from feelings of inadequacy, depression, loneliness, self-pity, and having to bear our own burdens.*

4. *Biblical hope is focused on the inheritance God has promised us in heaven. That inheritance is guaranteed for believers in Christ, so it won't disappoint us in the way all our earthly hopes ultimately will. If we hope for joy, peace, safety, or love, nothing and no one on earth can ultimately satisfy that hope. However, God will one day satisfy those hopes in heaven.*

5. *The present benefits of future-directed hope include an experience of God's Presence here on earth, answers to trust-filled prayers, and character qualities like joy and peace (because we're not consumed with worry).*

6. *Creation is waiting for God's children (all who believe in Jesus as their Lord and Savior) to be revealed. That is, it's waiting for Christians to be revealed in the glory they will have when they are fully transformed to be like Jesus in their character and with resurrected bodies like His.*

7. *Since the Fall in the Garden of Eden when sin entered the world, the earth has been in a state of decay. Earthquakes, droughts, and destructive storms are just some indications of creation's bondage, and it is the natural tendency of things to rot and crumble if energy isn't poured into maintaining them.*

8. *We will go into more detail on this in session 6, but the redemption of our bodies doesn't mean we are destined to be disembodied souls. Rather, we are destined to have redeemed bodies that don't suffer from disease, aging, or injury.*

9. *Hope isn't about what we already have; it is about relying on God's goodness to fulfill the promises He has made to us. It's important to understand this distinction so we don't grow impatient with waiting. Waiting is fundamental to hope.*

10. *Answers will vary. It's fine for this process to be unfamiliar at first. Again, be sure to keep track of time.*

11. *Answers will vary.*

12. *Answers will vary. Note that some people may find the silence intimidating at first. Anxiety can move each of us to fill the air with noise, but taking a moment to be silent before God is good for us. Let members express their discomfort, but make sure it is balanced by those who found the silence strengthening. Helping people become comfortable with silence will serve their private daily times with God in wonderful ways.*

13. *Take as much time as you can to pray for each other. You might have someone write down the prayer requests so you can keep track of answers to prayer.*

Session 2: Our Hope Is in God's Presence

1. *Answers will vary. For some people, heaven represents an everlasting church service or sitting on clouds with harps. For others, heaven represents a place where they will be reunited with believing loved ones and be continually in the Presence of God. Still others view heaven as a place where God will set them with challenging tasks to fulfill. It's okay if people are honest about having vague or even boring ideas of heaven. The next few sessions will give them a more robust and motivating picture of what they can look forward to.*

2. *In Ecclesiastes 3:11, God says that He has "set eternity in the human heart." As believers in Christ, we have an innate sense this world is not our true home—that we are "foreigners and exiles" on this earth (1 Peter 2:11) and that "our citizenship is in heaven" (Philippians 3:20). As we grow closer to God and spend time in His Presence, we long for the day when we will receive the promise of our eternal home.*

3. *Answers will vary. It's okay for the group members to admit they aren't aware of homesickness for heaven and that the longings they are aware of aren't obviously connected to heaven. By the end of this study, the group members will find it easier to see the connections.*

4. *As believers, knowing that nothing can prevent us from reaching our destination in heaven can significantly lessen our feelings of impatience and foster peace and joy. It can also help lessen the feeling that losses and disappointments in this life are catastrophic if we know that ultimately nothing on this earth can permanently harm us.*

5. *If we walk consciously with Jesus throughout the day, we are more likely to sense His Presence, which will be a great comfort to us. Walking with Christ also kindles in us the longing (hope) for a complete experience of His Presence face to Face. We get a little and become hungry for more.*

6. *John describes God in terms of gemstones because they best represent the beauty and light he witnessed of God's glorious Presence.*

7. *In the Old Testament, God appeared to the Israelites at Mount Sinai with "thunder and lightning, with a thick cloud over the mountain, and a very loud trumpet blast" (Exodus 19:16). These "flashes of lightning, rumblings and peals of thunder" in John's vision seem to suggest God's power and His holiness, which makes Him dangerous to approach if we are not purified by Jesus' righteousness.*

8. *In Exodus 33:20, God told Moses, "You may not look directly at My face [My glory], for no one may see me and live" (NKJV). However, when Jesus died on the cross, He took our sin on Himself and gave us His moral purity. By accepting this gift through faith, we are able to cross the gap between us and a holy God and enter into His holy Presence.*

9. *Worship is a central activity of heaven because it is the natural response of a rightly ordered soul to the Presence of God. It's what people in heaven want to do, and God deserves it. It should be something we want to do too as our souls become more and more rightly attuned.*

10. *Answers will vary. Note it's okay if people express they want to step back from such a holy God and the peals of His thunder. Hopefully they will also have a desire to behold a God who is more beautiful than precious gemstones.*

11. *Answers will vary.*

12. *Answers will vary.*

13. *Responses will vary.*

Session 3: Our Hope Is in God's Abundance

1. *Answers will vary. Some group members may have vivid memories of special meals they celebrated growing up, while others may not have as strong a recollection. The goal is to make people's imaginations of a banquet concrete, as it is easy for the idea of a heavenly banquet to seem vague or antiquated. You want the group members to move from their actual experiences of celebratory meals to the hard-to-imagine banquet of heaven.*

2. *Negative experiences can get in the way of our trusting that God's plans are to prosper His people. Talking through these experiences with other believers, praying, and anchoring ourselves in the truth of the Scriptures can help us clearly see God's plans are always for our benefit.*

3. *In John 15:4, Jesus told His disciples, "Remain in me, as I also remain in you. No branch can bear fruit by itself; it must remain in the vine. Neither can you bear fruit unless you remain in me." One way to remain in Christ and receive glimpses of our glorious future is simply to spend time alone with Him each day. We can also remain close to Christ by staying connected to those who also follow Him, taking time daily to study God's Word, actively serving others in love, and looking for ways to thank and praise Christ in whatever situation we find ourselves.*

4. *God displays His abundance through the variety and profusion of His creation in the natural world, and even in the universe. All the blessings and provisions in the world—right down to food, clothing, and shelter—are at His disposal, and He can give us anything we need.*

5. *A mindset of scarcity only leads to fear and an effort to control our world. A mindset of abundance leads to hope and trust. If we think of God as a God of abundance, we are more likely to be generous with our time and money, giving to others as God has given to us. We are more likely to be grateful for what we have rather than frustrated with what we don't have.*

6. *The food and aged wine symbolize the satisfaction of our every need and desire in heaven—not just barely enough, but abundantly.*

7. *It is important to picture people from all parts of the world at the heavenly banquet because God's promises are for all people regardless of gender, ethnicity, or race. God created diversity. He is preparing us not for uniformity but for unity and community while retaining our uniqueness.*

8. *Answers will vary, but certainly believing loved ones who have died will top the list. Group members may imagine people talking to one another, listening attentively to one another, enjoying each other's company, or enjoying the food. The point is to allow the Scripture to create a mental picture that fosters hope.*

9. *Even if we don't consciously feel smothered by the fear of death, it underlies the fears that do plague us—fears of not having enough to survive, fears of aging and disease, fears for our children.*

10. *Trusting in God is a fundamental quality He wants to form in us now, in preparation for heaven. Trust plays a role in preparing us for heaven because there can be no real relationship with God without trust. Hope requires trust.*

11. *Answers will vary.*

12. *Answers will vary.*

13. *Responses will vary.*

Session 4: Our Hope Is in God's Eternal Promises

1. *Answers will vary. One of the readings in this session will refer to hints of heaven in the present, and those hints of heaven may be things we are grateful for. We sometimes overlook those good things and only notice the things we're not grateful for, so this question gives members a chance to notice the good.*

2. *Eternity will be unrestricted ecstasy, seeing God face to Face and experiencing the full depths of his glory and love. Knowing that God has promised this eternity to those who believe in Him should fill us with confidence, hope, humility, and gratitude for His mercy toward us. The more we love God and remain close to Him, the more this promise fills us with joy.*

3. *In 1 Corinthians 13:11–12, Paul wrote, "When I was a child, I thought like a child, I reasoned like a child. When I became a man, I put the ways of childhood behind me. For now we see only a reflection as in a mirror; then we shall see face to face." We experience God's promise of eternity here and now by taking the time to be in His Presence, learn from Him, and mature in our faith. As we grow closer to God, we come to understand more of what this promise means to us and what hope it brings. It changes how we view our circumstances in life, for we know that one day when this life is over we will be with God in our eternal home.*

4. *Answers will vary. Seeing hints of heaven requires looking for them. Getting outside in a natural setting is helpful, though we can also see hints of heaven in people.*

5. *Walking along our life-path holding Jesus' hand refers to being in continual fellowship with Him and depending on Him. Short prayers all day long can help. Saying, "Jesus, I trust You," or just whispering His name can assure us of His Presence and keep us connected to Him.*

6. *Closeness to God, with no barriers caused by sin, is the greatest possible pleasure. If we really knew how glorious God is, we would feel that intensely.*

7. *Some group members may not be working through big losses or grief in their lives, but for those who are mourning, this will be a moving promise.*

8. *In John's day, gold and gemstones embodied the highest value and brilliance known to man. Not even the Roman emperor could build a city of gold and jewels.*

9. *We won't have to worry about sin and selfishness making friction out of personality differences. We will enjoy one another's differences instead of being annoyed by them. We also won't have any reason to fear our neighbors.*

10. *We can live with hope even if we are oppressed by ugliness or saddened by mourning and pain because we know these things will come to an end. If we have difficulty living with other people, we can look forward to a time when living with others will be a rich experience. These visions are meant to encourage us to persevere in hard circumstances.*

11. *Answers will vary.*

12. *Answers will vary.*

13. *Responses will vary.*

Session 5: Our Hope Is in the Earth's Transformation

1. *Answers will vary. The goal here is to bring group members' images and memories of the desert so vividly to mind that the Bible passage can strike them with the same force it did its first hearers. They would not have taken for granted the transformation of a desert.*

2. *Seeking perfection in this life can lead to frustration because nothing in this life will ever be perfect. We can never perform perfectly at work, our family relationships may never be as harmonious as we desire, and our desires for perfect bodies will be frustrated by aging and the limitations we were born with.*

3. *If we are too attached to other desires, we will inevitably live with disappointment or fear of disappointment. Desiring Jesus doesn't disappoint.*

4. *We can cultivate our desire for Christ by spending time with Him, talking with others about Him, reading the Bible, participating in worship of Him, and surrounding ourselves with visual or verbal reminders of Him.*

5. *Answers will vary. Make your group a safe place for people to be honest if they are struggling. If the response is all negative, though, you can invite people to talk about why they think the passages on heaven aren't making a bigger impact.*

6. *We can become more gripped by the hope of heaven by spending time deliberately thinking about what we know of heaven and reading the concrete information we are given in the Scriptures. We can ask God to make that information real to us and to quicken in us a longing for heaven. Talking with others about our rough road can help too, as can talking with them about heaven as concretely as possible. Saying things aloud will make the words and images stronger in our memories.*

7. *The desert shouts for joy when the desert plants bloom and the desert animals multiply. However, this is also poetry that evokes more than we can easily put into words.*

8. *The glory of the Lord is lush, vibrant, alive, and beautiful. It is not something static but a living magnificence like a tall cedar.*

9. *Answers will vary.*

10. *Isaiah says the highway will be a safe and sacred road on which the redeemed will travel toward the Holy City of Jerusalem. Isaiah has partly in mind the exiled people of Israel's journey back to the Promised Land after their captivity in Babylon. Our return to the Holy City will be like that.*

11. *Answers will vary.*

12. *Answers will vary.*

13. *Responses will vary.*

Session 6: Our Hope Is in the Resurrection

1. *Answers will vary. Sometimes people are surprised at how physically oriented the Bible is. They recognize hope for their souls, but not their bodies, and this attitude can be linked to a negative view of their bodies. So this question is intended to help group members value their bodies as God does. Some things to be grateful for include blood that is circulating properly and at the right pressure, nerves that are sending the right signals from hands and feet to the brain, and muscles that enable us to walk.*

2. *If we ask God to equip us with His living Presence, He will give us the strength to deal with whatever comes our way and give us the wisdom to make good decisions about our circumstances. His Presence is a foretaste of heaven that will foster our hope of more. He will enable us to see He is bigger than our problems, which will make us less likely to be sucked down into despair.*

3. *Let those group members who have tried leaning on God's strength and wisdom and seen the benefits encourage those who haven't tried it yet. You might talk about your own experience. Hebrews 11 lists many people whose stories are told elsewhere in the Bible, all of whom found that God was sufficient for them.*

4. *We need to lay aside activity and amusement—all of life's noise—for a time each day to focus on God's Presence. For instance, instead of turning on the television in the morning when we're getting ready for the day, we can spend that time in silence, turning our minds to God and the things on which He wants us to reflect. As we grow spiritually, we will increasingly choose to set our minds on God throughout the day rather than filling our thoughts with numbing, empty amusements.*

5. *Making time for God is essential in developing a certainty of His loving Presence during the dark times. A good pattern to establish is spending a chunk of time with God early in the day, and then moments throughout the day. If we can't see how to do that in our busy lives, it can be helpful to talk through our schedules with a friend or a group and come up with creative solutions. Invite group members to talk about some creative ways they can make space for God in their schedules.*

6. *Our bodies will be imperishable—they won't become disabled or diseased, and they won't die. They will be glorious, powerful, and animated by the Holy Spirit.*

7. *Answers will vary. We can only speculate what our spiritual bodies will do based on what we read in the Gospels of Jesus' resurrected body (see Matthew 28; Mark 16; Luke 24; John 20–21) and Paul's words in such passages as this one in 1 Corinthians 15. Some things our spiritual bodies might do that our natural bodies can't might include, for example, having certain abilities or knowledge we didn't have before. The point of the group imagining the possibilities is to kindle hope within them. The reality will be far better than we can imagine, not less than we can imagine.*

8. *So much of the franticness and dread of life on earth is driven by the fear of death—our own and that of our loved ones. Paul wants us, as fellow believers, to feel utterly safe—to know that nothing can ultimately harm us so that anxiety doesn't preoccupy us or hinder our courage to do all God asks. We are then free to love and serve God and others fully, without worry or distraction.*

9. *Though death is a tragedy, our hope of resurrection helps us understand that death within the family of God is not a catastrophe. We will see those loved ones again. Paul wants us to view death without fear.*

10. *Likewise, Paul wants us to face aging and disability without fear or dread. They are temporary. Beyond this earth is a life without them.*

11. *Answers will vary.*

12. *Answers will vary.*

13. *Responses will vary.*

Session 7: Our Hope Grows in Perseverance

1. *Answers will vary. Our childhood tendencies will largely be a matter of inborn temperament along with whatever messages our parents sent us about hard work and failure. Reinforce to the group that there's no condemnation for the way we were as children. It's helpful to be aware of this natural bent, however, because it affects how easily we respond to the Bible passage in this session, which urges us to cultivate the habit of perseverance. Some in your group will already be practiced at perseverance, while others will be facing a skill that doesn't come naturally.*

2. *Answers will vary. Helpful things include receiving encouragement from other people (such as those in the group), past experiences of God, and promises found in Scripture.*

3. *Answers will vary. Possible negative responses to despair include eating too much (or other addictions), watching too much television, surfing the Internet too much, and isolating too much from other people. More helpful responses include talking to a friend, praying, reading encouraging passages from the Bible and Christian books, and doing something constructive for another person.*

4. *Self-pity is a problem because once we give in to it a little, we tend to fall deeper and deeper into it. This can lead to depression and profound darkness.*

5. *The solution is to look past the self-pitying thoughts toward the light of God's Presence and to keep focusing on that light until God pulls us out of self-pity. One way we do this is by choosing to focus on the needs of others. As we take our eyes off our own problems and engage in the struggles other people are* *confronting, we begin to see our situation in a different light. Perhaps we come to understand, by comparison, that our own issues are not as great as they seemed. Or perhaps we come to realize we are not as alone in our struggles as we originally thought. Sharing our lives with others and focusing our thoughts on Christ enables us get a better perspective on our circumstances. It helps us realize that God is with us and is stronger than our problems.*

6. *When Paul says we should "boast" about the hope of seeing the glory of God, he doesn't mean we should be obnoxious about it. Rather, we are to tell others what we have experienced so they too can experience God's Presence. We do this not to win status for ourselves but to help others and honor God.*

7. *We glory in, or don't despise, our sufferings because the Bible says we need them to develop character and hope. We simply won't develop these qualities without suffering hardship.*

8. *Perseverance is continuing to try to do something despite obstacles, difficulties, and even failures along the way.*

9. *Our willing cooperation is reflected in our desire to endure, our determination to hold fast to our faith, our ability to welcome people into our lives who encourage perseverance rather than bitterness, and our openness to making time for God in our schedules. Cooperating with God also means being open to His work and His plans in our lives.*

10. *If we do not persevere and quit too easily, our failure is final and despair is the natural result. However, if we persevere, we foster the thinking that our failure isn't final, and we expect good to eventually come. Our thinking changes, and the results in our lives change. We are rewarded for perseverance, so it becomes a habit, part of our character. Long-range thinking toward heaven gets easier.*

11. *Answers will vary.*

12. *Answers will vary.*

13. *Responses will vary.*

Session 8: Our Hope Leads to Strength

1. *Answers for this final icebreaker question will vary. Use this discussion as a way for the members to reflect on the most important principle they took away from the study.*

2. *Waiting on the Lord means directing your attention toward Him in hopeful anticipation of what He will do and trusting Him with every fiber of your being, instead of trying to figure things out yourself. You wait on the Lord by carving out a chunk of time during your day to focus on Him rather than on other things, and even by taking a few moments to briefly turn your attention to the Lord in hopeful anticipation throughout the day. During such times you might just whisper a simple prayer such as, "I trust You, Jesus."*

3. *Answers will vary.*

4. *There are many ways that God represents the culmination of our hopes. For example, if we hope for freedom from anxiety, we are really hoping to experience the peace of God. If we hope for a fulfilling job, underneath that hope is the longing for joy, for feeling fully alive, which intimacy with God offers.*

5. *We know we're clinging to, or desperately attached to, one of God's gifts if thoughts of anxiety or anger arise when we think of losing it, or if we love that gift more than we love God, or if holding onto the gift gets in the way of our loving others, or if we are driven to try to control others in order to control the gift.*

6. *Isaiah says God can't be unjust—He created justice, He epitomizes justice, and His understanding is perfect even when we can't fathom it. Also, He is never too tired to grant justice. If something doesn't appear to be going our way, God must have a plan. Furthermore, He offers us strength to deal with our circumstances.*

7. *Answers will vary. Sometimes our anxiety is such that these truths seem abstract and don't penetrate to the place where our problems live. We can't force ourselves to respond to truth, but we can patiently keep reminding ourselves of truth. The Lord is the Creator, and He has control of our circumstances even when we don't. Continually bringing our minds back to this truth will eventually take the edge off anxiety and replace our despair with hope.*

8. *God promises to give strength and endurance to those who place their hope in Him.*

9. *This type of hope might involve crying out to God in prayer, letting go of frantic efforts to control outcomes, talking openly with God about our worries, memorizing Scripture, taking our thoughts captive, and deliberately making time for the Lord instead of staying constantly busy.*

10. *Answers will vary. If the group members have trouble putting words to their experience, set an example by putting words to your own. Think of a situation where you have struggled. How did hoping in the Lord help you? Or how did hoping in yourself or other people end up draining you of strength when other people or your own abilities let you down?*

11. *Answers will vary.*

12. *Answers will vary.*

13. *Responses will vary.*

ENJOY JESUS' PRESENCE.
FIND COMFORT
IN HIS PEACE.

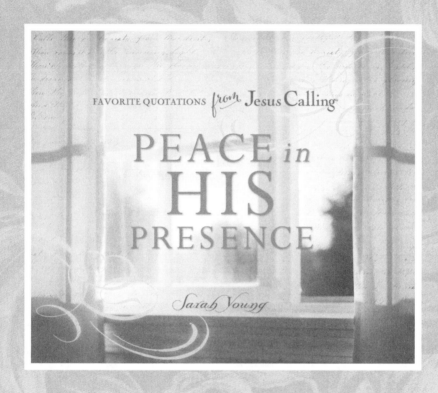

Selected quotes and scriptures from **Jesus Calling**
along with inspiring images will encourage you to
worship and find comfort in the peace of the Lord.

www.jesuscalling.com

Start a *Jesus Calling*® Book Club

The benefits of being part of a book club can be as varied as a group's members. It can act as a support network for its members and serve as a much needed sounding board for life's challenges. But the question is . . .

How do you get started?

At JesusCalling.com, you will find free book club resources specifically tailored for men and women using the devotional *Jesus Calling*, with new plans always being added.

Visit www.jesuscalling.com to start your book club today!

Facebook.com/**JesusCalling**   Twitter @**Jesus_Calling**   Instagram @**JesusCalling**

Google+ **Jesus Calling**   Pinterest **Jesus_Calling**